FROM *DARTH VADER AND SON* BY JEFFREY BROWN, PUBLISHED BY CHRONICLE BOOKS.
COPYRIGHT © 2013 BY LUCASFILM LTD & ® or ™ WHERE INDICATED.
ALL RIGHTS RESERVED. USED UNDER AUTHORIZATION.

PLACE
STAMP
HERE

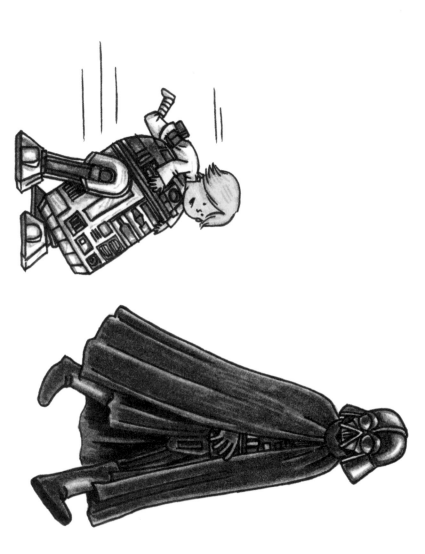

PLACE
STAMP
HERE

PLACE
STAMP
HERE

FROM DARTH VADER AND SON BY JEFFREY BROWN, PUBLISHED BY CHRONICLE BOOKS.
COPYRIGHT © 2013 BY LUCASFILM LTD & ® ™ WHERE INDICATED.
ALL RIGHTS RESERVED. USED UNDER AUTHORIZATION.

Research

APPRAISING EVIDENCE FOR NURSING PRACTICE

Ninth Edition

Denise F. Polit, PhD, FAAN
President, Humanalysis, Inc.
Saratoga Springs, New York
Professor, Griffith University School of Nursing
Brisbane, Australia
www.denisepolit.com

Cheryl Tatano Beck, DNSc, CNM, FAAN
Distinguished Professor, School of Nursing
University of Connecticut
Storrs, Connecticut

. Wolters Kluwer

Philadelphia • Baltimore • New York • London
Buenos Aires • Hong Kong • Sydney • Tokyo

Acquisitions Editor: Christina C. Burns
Product Director: Jennifer K. Forestieri
Development Editor: Meredith L. Brittain
Production Project Manager: Marian Bellus
Design Coordinator: Joan Wendt
Illustration Coordinator: Jennifer Clements
Manufacturing Coordinator: Karin Duffield
Prepress Vendor: Absolute Service, Inc.
9th edition

9 8 7 6 5 4 3 2 1

Printed in China

**Not authorised for sale in United States, Canada, Australia, New Zealand, Puerto Rico, and United
States Virgin Islands.**

Library of Congress Cataloging-in-Publication Data

Names: Polit, Denise F., author. | Beck, Cheryl Tatano, author.
Title: Essentials of nursing research : appraising evidence for nursing
  practice / Denise F. Polit, Cheryl Tatano Beck.
Description: Ninth edition. | Philadelphia : Wolters Kluwer Health, [2018] |
  Includes bibliographical references and index.
Identifiers: LCCN 2016043994 | ISBN 9781496351296
Subjects: | MESH: Nursing Research | Evidence-Based Nursing
Classification: LCC RT81.5 | NLM WY 20.5 | DDC 610.73072—dc23 LC record available at
https://lccn.loc.gov/2016043994

LWW.com

CCS1216

TO

Our Families—Our Husbands, Our Children (and Their Spouses/Fiancés),

and Our Grandchildren

Husbands: **Alan and Chuck**

Children: Alex (Maryanna), Alaine (Jeff), Lauren (Vadim), Norah (Chris),

Curt, and Lisa

Grandchildren: **Maren, Julia, Cormac, Ronan, and Cullen**

Denise F. Polit, PhD, FAAN, is an American health care researcher who is recognized internationally as an authority on research methods, statistics, and measurement. She received her Bachelor's degree from Wellesley College and her Ph.D. from Boston College. She is the president of a research consulting company, Humanalysis, Inc., in Saratoga Springs, New York, and professor at Griffith University, Brisbane, Australia. She has published in numerous journals and has written several award-winning textbooks. She has recently written a groundbreaking book on measurement in health, *Measurement and the Measurement of Change: A Primer for the Health Profession*s. Her research methods books with Dr. Cheryl Beck have been translated into French, Spanish, Portuguese, German, Chinese, and Japanese. She has been invited to give lectures and presentations in many countries, including Australia, India, Ireland, Denmark, Norway, South Africa, Turkey, Sweden, and the Philippines. Denise has lived in Saratoga Springs for 29 years and is active in the community. She has assisted numerous nonprofit organizations in designing surveys and analyzing survey data. Currently, she serves on the board of directors of the YMCA, Opera Saratoga, and the Saratoga Foundation.

Cheryl Tatano Beck, DNSc, CNM, FAAN, is a distinguished professor at the University of Connecticut, School of Nursing, with a joint appointment in the Department of Obstetrics and Gynecology at the School of Medicine. She received her master's degree in maternal–newborn nursing from Yale University and her doctor of nursing science degree from Boston University. She has received numerous awards such as the Association of Women's Health, Obstetric and Neonatal Nursing's Distinguished Professional Service Award, Eastern Nursing Research Society's Distinguished Researcher Award, the Distinguished Alumna Award from Yale University School of Nursing, and the Connecticut Nurses' Association's Diamond Jubilee Award for her contribution to nursing research. Over the past 30 years, Cheryl has focused her research efforts on developing a research program on postpartum mood and anxiety disorders. Based on the findings from her series of qualitative studies, Cheryl developed the Postpartum Depression Screening Scale (PDSS), which is published by Western Psychological Services. She is a prolific writer who has published over 150 journal articles. In addition to co-authoring award-winning research methods books with Denise Polit, Cheryl coauthored with Dr. Jeanne Driscoll *Postpartum Mood and Anxiety Disorders: A Clinician's Guide*, which received the 2006 American Journal of Nursing Book of the Year Award. In addition, Cheryl has published two other books: *Traumatic Childbirth* and *Routledge International Handbook of Qualitative Nursing Research*. Her most recent book is *Developing a Program of Research in Nursing*.